# ENGLISH UNWRAPPED

Lessons in Life and Language

*Lorraine Harnett*

ISBN: 978-1-5272-2289-2

www.englishunwrapped.com

This book is dedicated to all who read it

# Acknowledgements

Thank you to my family and friends for their love and patience.

Thank you to Marina Noriega Gutierréz, Alexandhros Printezis, Aneka Chomsomboon (Tam), Ali Karabacak, Ewan Jones, Elisiane Rae, Melanie Gail Mabhala, Fatima, Ivana and anonymous interviewees for providing personal suggestions and advice for readers.

Thank you to Helen Parker, Paul Boross, Felicity Cobbing, Nigel Paramor, Catherine Barnes, Joanne Kirkbright, Gary Butler, John and Jennifer Middleton, and Jane Upton for reading and advice.

Thank you to Ajay Sharma for writing the Foreword.

Thank you to David Rose for designing the cover.

Thank you for Matthew Houghton (mhdesigns@hotmail.co.uk) for typesetting the book.

# Foreword

I remember coming from India to work as a doctor in England. There were many English expressions that I didn't understand and things about living in England that I didn't know. For example, one day I was late for my work at the hospital because I didn't know that clocks are reset twice a year in England. A book like this would have helped me a lot!

I think this book will also help you, whether you are working here, seeking work, a student, refugee, asylum seeker, or a child, wife or husband of someone living here.

Whoever you are, if you are unfamiliar with the people and their customs, this book will be very useful for you.

Like most countries, there are different accents, expressions, humour and regional variations; I think this makes the English language adorable and to be celebrated. Lorraine does this in her book, making the book enjoyable to read.

*English Unwrapped: Lessons in Life and Language* contains information that you can use in your day to day life. It will help you to develop good communication, positive encounters and build bridges between people from diverse cultures and backgrounds.

Lorraine genuinely wants to help build bridges between people and help them to understand each other. As an English language teacher, she has worked with people from all over the world. She has listened to people and their stories, and this has helped her know what information is helpful to share with people who are not familiar with living in England. She is also aware of which words and phrases are most useful to know in day to day life. This advice is supported by quotes from people who have come to live and work in England. I would highly recommend this practical, easy to understand guide.

**Ajay Kumar Sharma** BSc (Honours), MBBS, MS, DNB, FRCS (Glas), FRCS (Edin), FRCS (General Surgery), Consultant Surgeon in Transplantation, Royal Liverpool University Hospital. Director of Core Surgical Training Merseyside, North-West of England Deanery. Associate Director of Postgraduate Courses in Transplantation, University of Liverpool. Regional advisor, Royal College of Physicians and Surgeons of Glasgow. Major AJ Sharma (Res), British Army.

# English Unwrapped

## Lessons in Life and Language

This guide is to give you a helping hand with life and language in England.

Life in England involves meeting different individuals, groups and communities. There are many established traditions, systems and laws, which reflect the history and cultural diversity of England. There are also new customs and emerging language and behaviours. Together we can start to understand these.

Actively using the English language (including body language and facial expressions), being polite and knowing about rights and responsibilities, may help you to be more happy, confident and safe.

# How to Use this Book

This guide refers to England. It does not cover the other countries in the UK (Northern Ireland, Wales and Scotland) or other UK territories. This is because they do not all have the same cultures, systems or laws.

The contents of this book are based on the author's experience of working with and interviewing people who have come to live in England from other countries. Within each section are quotations of advice provided by interviewees.

Each section covers an aspect of life that is fundamental to living in England, beginning with *Starting Off.* At the end of each section is a table of useful words and phrases with their meanings in the right-hand column. At the end of the book is a list of carefully selected non-commercial websites and telephone numbers.

The level of English needed to read this book is Intermediate to Upper Intermediate.

In any country the cultures, systems, laws and language change over time. For example, the impact of Brexit will lead to changes in English health and education systems, work eligibility and welfare, and some of these will be changed in law. Please check that you are reading the latest edition of this book. Please also refer to www.englishunwrapped.com where the author aims to provide accurate, up-to-date information.

# Contents

# 1. Starting Off

England is a country with 53 million people. People in England are either citizens, residents or visitors.

Local public services such as education, housing and waste management are managed by Local Authorities (sometimes known as, "The Council").

Crime prevention and enforcement are managed by local Police Services.

Healthcare is managed by the National Health Service (NHS).

Migration is managed by the Home Office (at a national level).

Work and unemployment support are managed nationally by the Department for Work and Pensions (DWP) and at a local level by Job Centre Plus.

Not all English people speak perfect English; there is a diversity of language and accents.

Body language and facial expressions, tone, pitch, and silence, combine to create meaning. To know and understand how the language is used helps with real communication.

*"When I first came, that time was the loneliest because I couldn't speak easily... I learned the most in those early days. Everyone should learn to speak English." Melanie*

Stereotypes of the English include polite manners, typically queuing and saying, "Please" and "Thank you". Not all English people share the same etiquette or identities, beliefs, attitudes and opportunities. Navigating through the subtle aspects of English life requires a willingness to observe both similarities and differences in people across the country.

> *"It's important to watch people. I started to learn about people by watching them, the way they spoke to each other, the way they behaved. I watched them. It's a good idea to observe people in the park, at the shops, on the bus and watch how the Brits do it! Be a social observer. I'm the sort of person who talks to strangers. In England, it's not always appropriate."*
> Melanie

**Please and thank you** are important words for communicating well in England. They cannot be over-used. These are the basics of English manners. It is polite to say, "Please" or "Thank you" in any situation where you ask or receive something.

> *"People here are quite polite, so you're going to want to be polite back ... always say, "Please" when asking for anything. People seem to be polite to everyone, including cleaners and train conductors.... It's fine, just say, "Pardon" if you don't understand someone. Don't say, "What?" That's quite rude."* Ewan

# Meet, greet and say goodbye

There are many ways to meet and greet people. A smile while saying, "Pleased to meet you" is risk-free. "How do you do?" is more formal. "Hello", "Hi" and "Good morning/ afternoon" are everyday greetings.

"How are you?" is a question greeting and the response is usually, "Fine, thank you". "Thanks" should never be used in formal situations and only be used if you know the other person uses, "Thanks". "Very well, thank you" is more formal. "How are you doing?" is informal and the response is, "Fine, thank you." Some people reply using the American English, "Good".

A very informal and youthful greeting, "Y'alright?" sounds like a question but it isn't. The response is, "Y'alright?".

Most initial meetings don't require physical contact. Shaking hands is more formal than a hug or a kiss. Refusing to shake someone's hand can be perceived as insulting. A general rule (we say, "rule of thumb") is to follow the other person's lead. If the other person offers their hand it's best to shake it, if they don't a smile is enough. Shake hands using the right hand. The number of cheek-kisses varies from 1-3. An initial awkward feeling soon passes.

*"Men and women mix freely. Women don't cover up their bodies. Even late at night in the winter on the streets, you can see women with hardly any clothes on. Not all women but some." Fatima*

Making and maintaining eye contact is believed to be a positive indicator of honesty and sincerity. It's also an indicator of listening and of respect. A nod of the head or sounds such as, "Hmm", "I see" or "Yes" also contribute to active listening. Whispering is considered rude. Winking can be perceived as "cheeky" or "flirtatious". In a small group situation it gives a good impression if eye contact is made with all of the people in the group.

**Being punctual** is polite. An apology is expected if you are late. Late means after the time agreed. A phone call or text with an estimated time of arrival (we say, "E.T.A.") is good manners. A brief explanation is fine unless you are asked for more detail. Being early isn't usually appropriate either, so the same rules apply. Certain places will not accommodate lateness, such as: theatres; car parks; the departure of buses, trains and aeroplanes; the Inland Revenue and Courts of Law. Schools and health services are disrupted by lateness but staff will appear calm and "professional". Friends and neighbours may regard lateness as selfish.

At social gatherings, "It's been lovely to meet you" is a standard phrase when people want to move on and meet other people. A polite smile, a slight step back (to provide personal space) and, "Lovely to meet you too" is a good response.

When saying "Goodbye" after a first meeting, it is pleasant to say, "It's been lovely to meet you" or "Nice to meet you". Thereafter, there are various ways to say goodbye including local expressions, "See you around", "Bye", "Take care". The key is to remember non-verbal communications: eye contact, smiling and nodding.

**Acceptable social conversations** tend to be about the weather, travel and holidays, family, sport and current surroundings. This is called, "small talk". To ask questions about a person's ill-health is not considered polite. A common question, "What do you do?", means, "What is your job?" and it is wise to remember that not everyone has a job and it can be very awkward if the person questioned is unemployed. "Where are you from?" is not very impolite but it is important to remember that people could have a complex mixture of ethnicity, nationality and background so this question may not evoke a simple answer. People who remember names and some details of previous conversations tend to establish rapport easily.

*"Be prepared for the weather. There are four seasons. People like to talk about the weather."*
*Elisiane*

Questions about personal finances (savings, income or cost of items) are generally regarded as rude or "nosey" (a "nosey parker" is someone who is overly interested in the affairs of others). Asking an adult their age is impolite. It is acceptable to ask a child their age. Comments about a person's weight-gain are likely to cause offence. Amongst females pointing out weight-loss is usually positive and is often used as a compliment. The boundaries for sexual or flirtatious comments are constantly changing and offence may be taken in either social or professional contexts.

Politics and religion are usually avoided unless between family and friends. Any homophobia, racism, misogyny or bigotry is usually veiled under polite expressions, such as, "It's common sense" or "I'm not racist but ..." or "In my day ...".

When people disagree they might say, "That's a bit harsh" or "I wouldn't put it quite like that". Alternative ways of disagreeing include, "I see what you're saying",

"I understand where you're coming from" and ironically, "With the greatest respect …". When someone says, "I'll bear it in mind", they usually mean that they won't.

Criticism of institutions and public services (especially the NHS), English food or weather may be expressed by English people but not by non-English. This also applies to the English national football and cricket teams. However, if making a formal complaint critical comments are necessary.

**Brexit**, the result of a referendum to leave the European Union, is a very sensitive issue. People have different opinions about it and emotions can be very intense.  It has divided some families and has damaged some friendships. Talking about Brexit in places of work, with strangers or in social gatherings is now considered a bit insensitive. Many English people will not talk about Brexit because it can create an awkward atmosphere. However, the freedom to hold a perspective and to express one's opinions (freedom of expression) is a very important principle: however, it is best to be careful, cautious and considerate when discussing this topic. It would be wise for a person who is not from the UK to listen to conversations about Brexit and speak with caution if offering direct opinions. This is an example of when facial expressions and body language can be the most beneficial. A slow nod of the head shows listening. Non-judgemental phrases include, "I hope it works out in the end". Questions that ask for clarification about any aspect of Brexit are unlikely to calm the atmosphere.

To say that someone is lying is a very big insult. Alternative phrases are, "I wouldn't put it like that" or "If you say so" or "That's one way of putting it". Informally, lies are called "porkies" or "fibs".

> *"I couldn't believe it when people who didn't know me started calling me, "love" and "darling". Taxi drivers or staff in a shop, they say, "thanks, babe" or, "thanks love," and it's normal, they're just being friendly."*
> *Marina*

**Personal space** is generally between 18–24 inches (46–61 centimetres). It's the physical distance that people need between each other to feel comfortable when they interact face to face. With a friend, the space may be less than with a professional. Surroundings affect how much space a person needs; the more the perceived risk, the more space people need. Anxious people tend to need more personal space. In a supermarket queue there should be space between the trolleys. It is unlikely that an English person will directly ask for more space. They are more likely to try to create it by leaning or stepping slightly away. Some people raise their voices if they want more personal space. Children are taught about personal space in the context of safety. It is considered inappropriate for an adult to touch a child who they do not know. There are no rules about walking or sitting next to or in front of older people. Males and females can socialise, dine, worship, work or study together.

**"In public"** means in a public place. Noise, such as shouting, swearing, playing loud music or videos, is considered ill-mannered in most public spaces. This includes when driving or using mobile phones. Mobile phones are generally turned to silent or flight mode during bus or train journeys, in restaurants, theatres and cinemas and in consultations with professionals. Some trains have "quiet zones" in which people are expected to be silent. There is huge variation in acceptable mobile phone etiquette.

**Saying sorry** is not always an admission of guilt, it is usually a recognition that something not quite right has happened.

> *"English people say sorry even when they've done nothing wrong. England is so quiet, people speak so quietly." Elisiane*

**Giving bad news** may start with, "I'm afraid …". The word, "afraid" when giving bad news is not about fear, it shows sympathy. Similar to, "sorry", "I'm afraid …" is a more gentle and polite way of giving bad news.

A cough is "caught" with one hand covering the mouth or by moving the mouth to the inner elbow.

A sneeze is "caught" in the elbow and is followed by saying, "Bless you" from anyone who has heard. Say, "Thank you" in return. It is polite to wash hands after an uncovered hand is used while coughing or sneezing.

Spitting, burping or nose-picking is considered very impolite.

Smoking is not allowed in many public places including most places of work.

Dropping litter/rubbish is illegal. It is regarded as unhealthy and inconsiderate. If bins are not available, items should be kept in a pocket or bag and taken home.

*"Listening to accents is very important. Use the TV, radio and films. Humour is not easy, so you can watch TV comedies and quiz shows. I thought I was speaking perfect English and then I came here and realised I knew nothing! Not all English people speak perfect English. Don't look down on people whose English isn't perfect. Don't worry, just improve yourself."* Ali

**Time** changes twice a year. Clocks go forward one hour at 01:00 on the last Sunday of March. Clocks go back one hour on the last Sunday in October. It is common to talk about the change in daylight hours around this time.

| Words and phrases | Meaning |
|---|---|
| Learn the ropes | Learn the basics of a new situation |
| Stand on your own two feet | Be independent, look after yourself |
| Pulling your leg/Taking the Micky | Only joking, trying to tease, making fun of someone |
| Live and let live | Everyone should be able to do as they please |
| When in Rome | People should try to fit in with local culture |
| Take your time | Do something at your own pace (can also be said with sarcasm if people are taking a long time to do something) |

| | |
|---|---|
| Common sense | A basic level of being sensible (though surprisingly not so common) |
| Count your blessings | Remember the good things that have happened in your life |
| Next of kin | The person most closely related to you. Usually the person to be telephoned in an emergency<br><br>Next of kin relates to inheritance issues also |
| Surname | Family name |
| Hunky dory | Things are ok/going well |
| You're one of us now | You're accepted into the group |

*"Hit the nail on the head" is an expression I often heard. It means, "Yes, exactly, that's exactly what I mean." Ali*

# 2. Making Friends

Friends have a personal relationship. They enjoy activities together, share feelings as well as possessions, help and support each other, keep promises and have the same understanding of what trust means. It isn't necessary to introduce friends to family or colleagues and doing this isn't a measure of friendship. A person's "best friend" is the person they value the most. Not everyone has one best friend.

*"There are lots of different people, different families, you meet all sorts." Ali*

*"You have to be open-minded. It's not worth getting upset easily, you have to see the best in people. You'll get accustomed to things." Elisiane*

People make friends with others who are at the same life-stage as them or who have shared interests or needs. Sharing the same neighbourhood or community also helps. Males and females can be friends with each other.

Popular places to make friends are: places of work; local parks; places of worship and cafes. Night classes, choirs, exercise groups and book clubs are increasingly popular. Information about clubs, classes, courses and events can be found in libraries, local newspapers, some public noticeboards or online. Virtual friendships can also be found online.

> *"I thought everyone would go to church for a Sunday mass. I was shocked to see how many people don't go to church."* Tam

> *"The churches are very small and empty and sometimes closed. I didn't expect there to be so many people who don't believe in God."* Elisiane

**Personal qualities** that are highly valued include modesty and sincerity. A person with these qualities may be called, "down to earth". Boastful arrogance and pretentiousness are generally disliked. Being called "simple" is offensive.

**Finger and hand gestures** that are offensive include, raising two fingers (index and middle) open with nails showing; we call this, "the V sign". It is also known as, "sticking two fingers up" or "flicking the Vs". Raising the middle finger with nail showing is equally offensive. Pointing to one's own temple in a circular movement means that you think the other person is crazy. Showing "thumbs up" is a good sign of appreciation or support.

**Gifts** such as flowers, chocolates or cake are usually welcome. A bottle of wine is a popular gift, where appropriate. Some communities do not approve of alcohol. Clothing should be avoided because people can be offended if the size is wrong. Political and religious gifts should be selected with care.

**Humour** can help to establish rapport (we say, "break the ice" about something that helps people to relax when starting a new relationship or scenario). Humour also affirms friendship groups, hides embarrassment, or faintly disguises disapproval while maintaining courtesy. The ability to laugh at oneself and at one's own mistakes is considered a good personal quality: it's considered undesirable if a person takes themselves too seriously. A "light-hearted" person is someone with a "good sense of humour" (GSOH). Even serious topics can be discussed with humour.  English humour may be a play on words (pun), sarcasm or irony. Figures of speech are used liberally. Humour may be morbid, ridicule others or be self-deprecating (putting oneself down). Making oneself a topic of humour (in other words laughing at oneself)

is typically English. It is probably because boastful

arrogance and pretentiousness are generally disliked.

*"Sometimes English people can be very jokey before they know you and they make fun of an idiosyncrasy … it can be seen as a provocation, I have seen this with many Italians, that they're not sure if it's serious or a joke." Alexandhros*

| Words and phrases | Meaning |
|---|---|
| Mate, chum, buddy, pal | Friend (informal) |
| Acquaintance | A person who is not a friend but who is personally known |
| Bump into | Meet someone without an arrangement |
| Put a face to a name | Meet someone who you haven't met but have either communicated with or heard about from someone else |
| With open arms | A genuinely enthusiastic welcome |
| Keep mum | Don't tell anyone the information, often used when someone's responsibility for an action is being hidden |
| Get on like a house on fire | Get on very well with someone |

| | |
|---|---|
| Fairweather friend | A person who is only friendly when things are going well |
| Man's best friend | His or her pet dog |
| Two peas in a pod | Two people who are very similar |
| Shoulder to cry on | Someone to listen to your problems |
| See eye to eye | To agree |
| Speak the same language | Have the same values and opinions |
| Singing from the same hymn sheet | To have a shared understanding, saying the same thing |

*"People say, do you need a hand? They mean, do you need help." Elisiane*

# 3. Homes

**Homes** are usually a house or a flat and can be temporary or permanent. Prices vary in England, with London being the most expensive place to live.

> *"You can get ten miles away and hear a totally different accent. It's the same with house prices; it depends where you are."* Ali

**To rent**, a deposit and a reference from a previous landlord are usually required.

> *"You need a deposit before you can rent a flat. You need references as well."* Marina

**To buy** a home with a mortgage, you will need to provide evidence of your income and a deposit.

**Utilities** (water, electricity, gas, internet) are supplied by private companies. Some research will help to find the best provider. English homes usually have central heating for the colder months. Homes have carpets or wooden floors for the same reason.

> *"England, how cold it is! England is so cold, I had to learn how to use a radiator."* Tam

**Sharing accommodation** can be done with friends (flatmates/housemates) or family members. It is not uncommon for a mixture of male and female friends to share accommodation. The average age to get married in England is 30-32. It is not uncommon for people to live with their intended spouse before their marriage and they are called, "partners".

**Neighbours** may or may not be friendly. It depends on the people and the area.

> *"Neighbours can be lovely. I was lucky. I give my spare key to my neighbour and I have hers. We take packages for each other as well."* Fatima

**Visiting** a person's home without an invitation or a specific purpose is usually impolite. "Pop 'round any time" doesn't usually mean this. It's the same as, "You must come 'round for dinner". It is not always an invitation to dinner; it may just be friendliness.

> "At first I didn't realise that it is polite to telephone before visiting someone at home. Now, I prefer it, I really like having time to tidy the house before people arrive!" Melanie

**Marriage and divorce** can be between same-sex or opposite-sex couples. Only one spouse is permitted at any time.

**The most common pets** are dogs – around a quarter of English people have a pet dog. Pets are not ordinarily allowed in rented accommodation. Other popular pets are cats, fish, guinea pigs and caged birds. Pets are often referred to as "part of the family", with special beds, toys, birthdays, health insurance and treats.

**Noise** from home maintenance such as drilling, hammering or lawn-mowing is avoided after 20:00 and before 08:00 and is not welcomed on Sunday mornings.

**Waste and recycling** are managed by Local Authorities. Various bins (for food, plastics, papers, bottles etc.) are provided for collections on specific days of the week. Residents are expected to put their bins out on the pavement outside their home on the correct collection day. Disposal of large or heavy items requires an appointment for collection. Alternatively, local Household Waste Centres will dispose of most items.

**Parking a car** can be a delicate matter. It is courteous not to park in front of another's front door without permission. It is neighbourly to park outside your own home, on a road away from people's front doors or in a car park, if possible.

**A Television Licence** is needed by all TV viewers except people who are 75 years or over. Viewers who only download content after broadcast still need to buy a TV licence for any device.

*"TV cooking shows can be fun and useful especially for women alone at home. I was a bit scared of going out shopping alone and I only had a few things in the cupboard. The show where they made dinners from very few ingredients helped me a lot and I thought, I could make a meal with very little too! I'm sure they have no idea how important their show was for me. Find a TV programme that you enjoy. Quiz shows use a lot of English phrases. If you're in London, watch EastEnders and if you're in Manchester or the North West, watch Coronation Street, it'll help with the accents."* Melanie

| Words and phrases | Meaning |
|---|---|
| Address | Details where a house or business is situated |
| Postcode | A list of numbers and letters at the end of an address |
| Estate Agent | Agent for buying and selling places to live |
| House owner | Person/s who own or are buying the house |
| Mortgage | Loan from a bank to buy a house |
| Letting Agent | Agent for renting and letting places |
| To rent (verb) | To lease/hire |
| Rent (noun) | Regular payment |
| Flatmate/housemate | Person who shares house/ flat with others |

| Landlord | Person who allows people to have a house/flat in exchange for a sum of money paid regularly |
|---|---|
| Under the same roof | Sharing the same home |
| Home-sick | Nostalgia, longing for home |
| Safe as houses | Very safe |
| Behind closed doors | Privately within the home |
| Make yourself at home | Welcome. Please feel as comfortable here as you would in your own home |
| A man's home is his castle | A person's own rules apply in their own home. It is a place of refuge and safety |
| My place | My home |

*"This is my dream house. My dream house is a big one to fit our family in a nice, calm place. I don't like big cities." Elisiane*

# 4. Work

*"I got a job through a job agency [recruitment agency] once I got here."* Ali

**People eligible to work in England** (without a work visa) are UK, European Economic Area (EEA) citizens and Swiss Nationals. You must be 16 years old or over. Everyone else, including religious and charity workers, needs to apply for a visa. Fees vary. Detailed information is on the UK government website (online link provided at the end of this book). Information required may include passport/travel identification, proof of savings and immunisations.

Income Tax and National Insurance (NI) are taken from workers' pay by employers who then transfer it to the government. Both are calculated according to how much a person is paid. In order to calculate the correct amount, a unique lifelong NI number is provided. This can only be applied for from within the UK and a UK address is required. Telephone support numbers are on the government website. A face-to-face interview usually finalises the process. People are allowed to work for a maximum of 9 weeks before an NI number has been provided to them.

*"You need a National Insurance number for work."*
*Marina*

Asylum seekers should provide employers with an Application Registration Card (which states eligibility to work), National Insurance number (NI) and name. Refugees provide their Biometric Residence Permit, Immigration Status Document (ISD), NI and name.

A CV (Curriculum Vitae) does not need to include your age, gender or have a photograph; this information is optional. Applications for work do not always get a reply.

England has a national minimum wage for people aged 16 years and over. There is a minimum living wage for people over the age of 25 years. This applies to foreign workers. It can be calculated online. Minimum and living wages do not apply to volunteers or self-employed people.

"Office hours" are the standard working week: often Monday to Friday 09:00-17:00. Weekends are Saturdays and Sundays. A person's hours of work will vary according to their role and the organisation for which they work.

*"I find the people are very punctual for work." Elisiane*

Men and women can work together as equals.

*"My first shock was in my first job – I couldn't believe the bad language [swearing]. I'd never met these people before, women shouting at men, I heard it all night, I was shocked." Ali*

**Professional conduct** means maintaining calm and respectful words and behaviour towards colleagues and clients. Start with, "With all due respect …" when giving a criticism or disagreeing with someone.

Trustworthiness and discretion are very important personal qualities in the workplace.

**Managers** and superiors may use expressions that have more than one meaning. For example, "It's fine" may mean it's fine but could also mean, "It's really bad". Attentive listening to tone and seeing facial expressions can help to understand the intended meaning.

When a manager says, "If you say so" it usually means, "You do not know what you are talking about."

It is common for managers to do the tasks that staff do. It is considered a positive thing and is known as "mucking-in".

*"In my experience, managers can do the worker's work. They can help the workers. It's normal." Marina*

Flirting and sexual behaviours at work are considered unprofessional. Having sexist, racist, homophobic, bigoted or violent views is unacceptable in a work environment. Unauthorised use of the internet and social media are increasingly reprimanded. Refusal to do tasks, being aggressive or cheating is usually not tolerated by superiors. Bullying, swearing and age discrimination are not allowed, although sometimes tolerated. Some organisations have a written Code of Conduct within an Employee Handbook.

> *"People say, "love" and "sweetheart" like, "Can I help you, love" or "Well done, sweetheart" but it's very inappropriate at work in a professional setting."*
> *Melanie*

**Volunteering** is generally considered a positive activity. Reasons English people volunteer include: enjoying supporting people or places, improving something in the community, enhancing a CV (Curriculum Vitae), meeting people, making friends and socialising.

The differences between volunteering and voluntary work are sometimes unclear amongst English people and organisations. It is known as a "*grey area*" when something is vague.

**Voluntary work** means that there is an agreed activity, done at an agreed time and is rewarded through money or another payment instead of cash, such as training, experience, discount, childcare or living allowance. Some voluntary workers are entitled to the national minimum wage. Voluntary work may or may not be for a charity. Examples are internships and jobs with private employers who expect training and qualifications to be achieved and for the worker to work regular hours. **Eligibility criteria for voluntary work** state that there is no minimum age but many organisations cannot get insurance for under 16-year-olds to do voluntary work. There is no maximum age limit but insurance may not cover people over 80 years. EEU and Swiss Nationals can do paid or unpaid work. People outside the EEU and Switzerland need to apply for a one-year visa to do voluntary work/charity work.

*"You'll always hear people asking if you want a cup of tea. It's like everyone joins in with tea. They say, a cuppa. It's like it's a group thing, it makes you part of the team." Elisiane*

| Words and phrases | Meaning |
|---|---|
| Visa | A stamp and a note in a passport that confirms conditions of entry into a country including eligibility to work |
| Job description | List of things that someone must do in their job |
| Probation | Period of time to see if someone can do the job properly. Until the end of a probation period, the job is temporary |
| Job-share | Arrangement for two people to share the work and pay of one job |
| Hot-desking | Sharing one or more desks with others |
| Confidential | To be kept secret. Do not tell anyone. Also, 'in confidence' or 'strictly confidential' |
| Minimum Wage (National Minimum Wage) | Minimum pay per hour for paid workers. Determined by age. Exceptions are students on placement, some voluntary workers, some government schemes e.g. apprenticeships, school-age children. Calculated for workers at www.gov.uk/am-i-getting-minimum-wage Calculated for employers at www.gov.uk/minimum-wage-calculator-employer |

| | |
|---|---|
| Living Wage (National Living Wage) | Minimum pay per hour for paid workers over 25 years of age.<br><br>Exceptions are students on placement, some voluntary workers, some government schemes.<br><br>Calculated for workers at <u>www.gov.uk/am-i-getting-minimum-wage</u><br><br>Calculated for employers at **<u>www.gov.uk/minimum-wage-calculator-employer</u>** |
| Bank holiday | Public holiday. These are listed on the government website. Diaries usually identify public holiday dates |
| Portfolio working | Working for more than one employer at any one time (there is an increasing trend towards this in England) |
| Professional behaviour/manner | A written or unwritten code of behaviour that is appropriate for the work role |
| Pull a sicky | To pretend to be unwell and to take time off work. It is considered a bad lie |
| Get the ball rolling | Start something |
| Keeping my head down | Saying as little as possible to avoid confrontation |
| Keep me in the loop | Tell me about any relevant information |
| Off the record | Do not repeat publicly (during formal meetings – do not record this in the minutes) |
| The bottom-line | The most important feature |

| Big cheese | Most senior decision maker. A very important person |
| --- | --- |
| Snowed under | Very busy |
| Bring home the bacon | Earn money for the family |
| Charity | An organisation for people or places who need help. Charities are also known as, voluntary organisations, non-governmental organisations (NGOs) |
| Payment-in-kind | Activity rewarded through anything other than cash |
| Grey area | Something that is vague |

*"Someone at work told me to use elbow-grease and I asked them, "Where do I get it from?" They all laughed! Elbow-grease means to put more effort into something, like you are scrubbing or polishing." Ali*

*"Once I had a workman at my house and I asked him to do an extra job for me. He said, "I don't do foreigners" and I thought he meant that he wouldn't do it for me because I was a foreigner. I said racism is illegal and he apologised, laughed and explained that a foreigner means an extra job in addition to a main job!" Ali*

*"When my manager said, "I would do that", I thought he meant that he would do it. "What a helpful guy!" I thought. What he actually meant was that he thought I should do it. It was his way of telling me to do it." Anon.*

# 5. Childcare and Education

**Childminders** are individuals who are registered to look after babies and children.

**Babysitters** are usually arranged informally, but may be arranged through a childcare business. There is no legal minimum age for a person to babysit.

**Day nurseries**, playgroups and nursery schools are registered to look after babies and children before they start school. All have qualified staff and local opening times and payment arrangements. These are open during the daytime.

**Afterschool clubs** look after children when the school day ends, until parents collect, usually until 18:00.

**The English School System** mandates that all children must have an education between the age of five and 16 years. This can be either at school or home. The majority of children start to go to school in the academic year of their 5<sup>th</sup> birthday. Further study (school, home, or college), training or work is compulsory between 16-18 years.

"In loco parentis" means, "in place of a parent". The law is that organisations such as schools, colleges and universities have a duty to do what they believe is in the best interests of the children in their care.

Primary schools educate children for the first seven years; secondary school (sometimes known as high school) thereafter. Books and stationery are provided in primary schools. In secondary school students are expected to provide their own stationery. Most schools have a uniform. The academic year is September to July and is usually divided into three terms, with holidays in-between. It's traditional for children not to like school dinners but the majority of children in England eat them.

Apart from independent schools (i.e. public and private schools), English schools are free of charge. Applications are made online or to the Local Authority.

> *"People don't call school teachers by their first names. It's Mr or Mrs here and you are respectful. Be very polite."* Fatima

**State-funded schools** accept children from UK, EEA (European Economic Area) and Switzerland in accordance with each school's Admissions Code. Child asylum seekers and refugees have the same rights. Children who are with a parent or guardian who is an overseas national and has a visa are usually entitled (tourist and short-term study visa holders are not entitled). Children on short-term holidays cannot temporarily attend a state-funded school. The UK Home Office handles applications. Doubts about immigration status are not reasonable grounds for a school to refuse entry. Some children from non-EEA countries may only attend a fee-paying independent school.

**Short-term study visas and Tier 4 Student visas** are provided for students who have been accepted to an independent school, English language school, further or higher education. Information required may include passport/travel identification, proof of financial savings/ support and immunisations.

## School year groups

| Age | Year |
|------|-----------|
| 4-5 | Reception |
| 5-6 | 1 |
| 6-7 | 2 |
| 7-8 | 3 |
| 8-9 | 4 |
| 9-10 | 5 |
| 10-11 | 6 |
| 11-12 | 7 |
| 12-13 | 8 |
| 13-14 | 9 |
| 14-15 | 10 |
| 15-16 | 11 |
| 16-17 | 12 |
| 17-18 | 13 |

*"School children are not automatically considered stupid if they are struggling. In England, the teachers really look after children. Kids aren't humiliated in school." Melanie*

# Exams and tests

Internal tests and exams take place in schools throughout the academic year.

National exams are:

SATs in years 2 and 6 (a test that measures reading, writing and math levels in state schools)

GCSE in year 11 (General Certificate of Secondary Education)

'A' level in year 13 (Advanced level)

Applications for university are made with the support of schools through the Universities and Colleges Admissions Service (UCAS).

| Words and phrases | Meaning |
| --- | --- |
| National Curriculum | List of subjects that children learn in England. Private schools and academies are not legally bound and don't have to follow this |
| Co-educational (Co-ed) school | School for male, female and transgender together |
| Single-sex school | School for either boys or girls |
| Phonics | A popular method of teaching reading with sounds and symbols |
| Special Educational Needs (SEN) | The needs of a child who has a learning difficulty or disability. Special educational needs co-ordinators (SENCO) provide support in nurseries, schools and further education colleges |
| Parent-Teacher Association (PTA) | Organisations attached to each school to get parents involved in school fundraising. The school secretary has details of meetings |
| Parents Evening | An evening of short meetings between parent/s and teacher/s about a child's progress at school. Some schools encourage children to attend and others do not. The school secretary will advise |
| Office for Standards in Education, Children's Services and Skills (OFSTED) | Inspects and reports on state schools (available online) |

| | |
|---|---|
| Non-uniform Day | A day when children do not wear their uniform to school. Most schools encourage donation for charity on these days |
| Sports Day | A school afternoon or morning with outdoor races for children. Parents are usually welcome |
| In-service Training Day (Inset day) | Teacher planning and development days. Schools are closed to children |
| Bookworm | Someone who reads a lot |
| Learn off-by-heart | To memorise and recall something |
| The Three Rs/3Rs | Reading, writing and mathematics |

*"They said my daughter was "teacher's pet" and we were upset, we thought it was rude to speak of her as an animal. We didn't need to be upset, it means to be teacher's favourite student." Anon.*

# 6. Health and Healthcare

The National Health Service (NHS) provides healthcare.

It is paid for by taxes and fees from overseas patients.

Some services are free and others are not. All services

are monitored and regulated, for example by the Care

Quality Commission, Department of Health, General

Medical Council, the General Dental Council or

Healthwatch.

Private healthcare is also offered by businesses that

provide screening, vaccinations, operations and some

treatments. Costs vary. All services are regulated by the

Care Quality Commission.

**Community Health Services** provide every person

(citizen, resident or visitor) in England the opportunity to

be seen by a community doctor or nurse free of charge.

A community doctor is known as a General Practitioner

(GP).  Physical and/or mental health may be discussed.

Everything discussed with a health professional remains

confidential unless the patient is at risk of harm to themselves or others. Telephone or visit a General Practice (also known as Doctor's Surgery) to register and to make an appointment.

> *"Doctors in England ask a lot more about patient's lifestyles, like about how much you smoke, how much you drink and such a lot of detail about how many units of alcohol a day, a week..." Marina*

To register, complete the General Registration Form which can be found at any General Practice. Date of Birth is recorded as dd/mm/yyyy. Age starts at the date of birth. There is no minimum length of stay in England before a person can register with a GP. ID and proof of address are asked for but are not compulsory and not having them is not reasonable grounds to refuse a registration. If a person does not have an NHS number, they can still register with a GP. If you move house you can register with a GP in your new area.

It is at the discretion of the General Practice whether the patient will be a "temporary" or "permanent" patient. "Temporary" is if the person is staying locally for more than 24 hours and less than 3 months. "Permanent" is for people staying more than 3 months. It is not uncommon for a General Practice to provide temporary status for people who are not from the UK if they cannot provide proof of address. Permanent patient status is usually provided once the documents are provided.

Nationality or immigration status are not reasonable grounds to refuse registration with a General Practice. The same rules apply whether the person is a worker, job-seeker, student, refugee, asylum seeker, adult or child.

Patients, including children, are expected to explain their symptoms themselves if they can. It is normal for a GP or community nurse to ask questions about lifestyle (smoking, drinking alcohol, exercise etc), but the patient can choose whether to answer or not.

**Hospital care** is given when a GP refers a patient for specialist care or if the patient enters as an emergency. Overseas adults may be charged for specialist care. No-one is charged for emergency treatment or treatment of certain infectious diseases unless admitted as an inpatient. Inpatient and outpatient care may be chargeable. Ambulances are used to take patients to the hospital for emergency care. EU and Swiss Nationals are encouraged to present their EHIC card to cover health care expenses. Some visas require payment of a health surcharge. The hospital's overseas visitor manager is responsible for recovering the costs of care provided in a hospital. Patients without insurance may be charged 150% of the NHS tariff for their treatment.

**Dispensing chemists** provide healthcare advice free of charge. Some adults must pay for the dispensing of prescriptions at a rate of £8.60 per item. Others are exempt. Contraception on prescription is free of charge.

UK childhood vaccinations are free of charge and are

administered between the ages of eight weeks and 14 years. Vaccinations for 65-year-olds and above are also free of charge. Some travel vaccinations must be paid for.

Immediate, necessary and urgent care is provided free of charge regardless of nationality, patient or immigration status.

*"I am training to be a nurse and this quote by Maya Angelou [and attributed to others] is why I want to communicate properly with my patients. 'I've learned that people will forget what you said, people will forget what you did, but people will never forget how you made them feel.' " Anon.*

| Words and phrases | Meaning |
| --- | --- |
| Quack | Doctor (slang) |
| Just what the doctor ordered | Exactly what is needed – usually to improve health (not literally a doctor's advice) |
| Check-up/MOT | Health check |
| Ache | Persistent mild pain |
| Run down | Poor health, generally weak |
| Under the weather | Poor health, slight illness |
| Off colour | Poor health appearance especially pale in the face |

| Come down (with something) | Become unwell |
|---|---|
| Right as rain | Excellent health |
| As fit as a fiddle | Excellent health |
| Full of beans | Lots of energy |
| Spare tyre | Roll of flesh around the waist |
| Runs in the family | Common family trait or condition |
| Throw-up | Vomit/sick |
| Blue | Sad |
| Dropping like flies | Large numbers of people are getting sick |
| Sick | Feeling unwell (also used by young people to mean "good") |

*"When I'm tired, I need to "recharge my batteries". It's a good way of saying to get some rest." Fatima*

# 7. Community Safety and the Law

*"It's quite safe here. You always want to be in a group at night, just to be safe. A group of two or more seems to be what most people do." Ewan*

**The age of criminal responsibility** is 10 years. This is the age a person is presumed able to be responsible for a crime. A child is anyone under 18 years (before their 18th birthday).

**"Innocent until proven guilty"** means that every person is presumed innocent of a crime until they have been convicted of that specific crime in a fair trial. This is the law.

**"Freedom of speech"** means anyone can express their opinions, as long as they don't motivate violence or hatred. This is the same for social media and any part of the virtual environment.

**Births, deaths, civil partnerships, marriages, change of name, change of gender** must be registered with a local register office (part of the Local Authority).

# Police powers

There is no requirement to carry ID in England. Police can stop anyone in a public place and ask why they are there, where they have travelled from, what they are doing, saying or carrying and why. When the police ask for an explanation it is not illegal to refuse to provide personal details (name, age, address etc.) but anyone who is questioned is expected to account for their actions.

People from outside of the UK have the right to inform their embassy, consulate or high commission if they are detained by the police. Children detained before they reach 17 years (before their 17th birthday) should not be interviewed without a parent/legal guardian or appropriate adult. Language translators should be provided if the first language of the child or accompanying adult is not English.

*"People should know that police officers don't have guns. We were shocked. I said to my husband, look at them, they don't even have any weapons on them."*
*Melanie*

**Discrimination** is illegal. The police (and other services such as the NHS) are not allowed to discriminate based on any of the following:

• age

• disability

• gender reassignment

• marriage and civil partnership

• pregnancy and maternity

• race

• religion or belief

• sex and sexual orientation

*"My confidence grew when I said to myself, I am here legally and I pay my taxes. It's important to believe in yourself. As a foreigner, you can ask for respect. No one is superior to you. It's the law. You are somebody who deserves the same that everyone has."* *Melanie*

The legal age to have sex is 16 years. This is known as "the age of consent." Anyone younger is referred to as 'underage' or 'a minor'.

To protect 16 and 17 year-olds, it is also illegal:

• to take, show or distribute indecent photographs

• to pay for or arrange sexual services

• for a person in a position of trust to engage in sexual activity

It is illegal to smoke or vape under the age of 16. The police can confiscate smoking products from under 16-year-olds. It is illegal to buy cigarettes, tobacco, e-cigarettes or e-liquid under 18 years.

The minimum age to drive a vehicle is 17 years.

The minimum age to join the British Armed Forces or Reserves (formerly Territorial Army) is 16 years. Before their 18th birthday, children need consent from parent/s or guardian/s. Non-UK citizenship holders from Ireland, the Nepalese Gurkhas or people from Commonwealth countries with five years of residency in the UK or indefinite leave to remain may also apply to join. The maximum age varies.

The minimum age to get married is 16 years. Before their 18th birthday, children need consent from parent/s or guardian/s.

Marriage between certain close relatives is not allowed.

Children are allowed to drink alcohol at home (or at other private homes) with their parent's permission. The law for providing alcohol to other people's children is unclear. The minimum age to buy alcohol is 18 years. A 16-year-old can drink alcohol in licensed premises (pub, bar, hotel, restaurant) if accompanied by an adult who buys the drink and if they are having a meal. Police can confiscate alcohol from anyone (any age) if they think a child is involved.

**Retailers** are not allowed to sell the following items to anyone under 18 years old: alcohol, fireworks and other explosive devices, DVDs, videos and games certified as 18, solvents (if retailer believes the child may inhale it), butane, knives, axes and razor blades.

**Sales** of Lottery Tickets are restricted to people 16 years and over.

# Driving

English road users drive on the left. It is illegal to drive without a licence and vehicle insurance. Some are temporarily transferrable from other countries. An MOT (vehicle safety test) is required for cars more than three years old. The Driving and Vehicle Licensing Agency (DVLA) oversees these. "The Highway Code" provides more information.

*"My advice is, remember to look right when crossing the road!" Marina*

Seat belts are mandatory. Children must use a child car seat until they're 12 years old or 135cm tall, whichever comes first.

Car horns are used for alerting others to danger (although sometimes used for random purposes). Overuse of horns is considered antagonistic in most circumstances but especially in places such as school car parks and residential areas.

*"The first thing I noticed was the cleanliness of the roads." Tam*

## Cycling

Cycle lanes are specifically provided to improve the journeys of cyclists. Bicycles should be in good condition with brakes and lights. It is not compulsory to wear a helmet. It is not illegal to use mobile phones when cycling but you could be charged with a 'not-paying-due-care-and-attention' offence. Cycling is not allowed on motorways or on pavements. "The Highway Code" provides more information.

## Safeguarding

Harming children or adults is illegal. This includes neglect, physical, sexual, emotional and psychological harm. Family beliefs, cultural considerations or financial incentives do not override this law.

People working for: the police; education establishments (universities, colleges and schools); health services (community, primary and secondary care); local authorities (including social care services) and charitable organisations, are expected to report any concern that they have about a child or vulnerable adult's safety.

The police, NHS, local authorities (including social services), and educational services are responsible for making enquiries to safeguard and secure the welfare of any child or vulnerable adult who is suffering (or likely to suffer) harm or neglect.

| Words and phrases | Meaning |
|---|---|
| Illegal | Against the law, not legal, unlawful |
| Break the law | Do something unlawful |
| Offender, criminal, culprit | Person who has been found guilty of breaking the law |
| Have a brush with the law | Have a brief experience with the police (as an offender) |
| Bobby (slang), Cops (slang), Pigs (slang), Old Bill (slang), "filth" (slang) | Policeman/woman |

| In the dock | In court |
| --- | --- |
| Crown Court | Place of trial with a jury |
| Magistrates Court | Place of trial without a jury |
| Serving time | Spend time in prison |
| Behind bars | In jail (short term)/prison (longer term) |
| If you can't serve the time, don't do the crime | If you are unable cope with prison, you shouldn't have done the illegal act |
| Get away with murder | Do something bad without being punished (not literally murder) |
| Bend the rules | Slightly change the rules (not in a harmful way) |
| Clean up your act | Improve your behaviour |

*"I heard, "Sod's Law". It means if something can go wrong, it will. Quite a bit of negative thinking." Fatima*

# 8. Children

Children are sometimes encouraged to call adult friends "auntie" or "uncle" even if they are not related. It is normal for adults to be called by their first name by their friends' children. However, it is more traditional to be called by prefix 'Mr', 'Miss' or 'Mrs' before the family name.

Children tend to make friends in their neighbourhood; at local clubs, groups, classes and events, as well as through school, at the local park or playground, place of worship, fitness centre or café.

Information about local activities can be found on noticeboards in shops and post-offices. Community centres and libraries also have information about activities and some of these will be for parents and children. For an online search, use terms such as, "mother and baby", "parent and toddler", "things to do for teenagers" and add the local area name (council name or neighbourhood name) or specify an activity/sport.

It is acceptable to ask other parents about activities that their children are involved with. Offering to help with taking and collecting children is considered friendly and provides an opportunity for children to be together.

Some activities are free of charge and some need to be paid for. Some need pre-booking and others are "drop-in" ("drop-in" means that you can arrive without booking in advance).

Complimenting a child on their appearance is usually done through the adults and is a sign of approval. Examples of compliments include, "They're a credit to you" meaning that their manners are good. "They'll break some hearts" meaning that they are very beautiful/ handsome. Less positive examples are, "They keep you on your toes" meaning their behaviour is unpredictable and anything might happen.

# Parties and gifts

**A party invitation** may be a card, letter or text message. Teenagers usually arrange their own invitations. It is polite to reply. It is considered impolite not to reply, even if you cannot attend. The phone number or email address is usually provided on the invitation next to "RSVP". RSVP translates to, "répondez s'il vous plaît" in French, meaning, "please reply."

Parents make their own arrangements to take and collect young children from parties; the host doesn't usually provide transport. When very young, at least one parent/ guardian usually stays with the child. As children grow, parents only stay if they are invited. It is polite to offer to help but equally important to respect the host's reply. It is normal to leave a parent's mobile phone number with the host parent and considered polite to be on-time for arrival and collection.

A suitable gift is one that doesn't offend. Knives and guns, or anything that shoots projectiles, are likely to be unwelcome. Consider avoiding anything that makes a particularly loud or irritating sound. Religious or political gifts can be easily misunderstood. Make-up for very young children is not considered age-appropriate.

If uncertain how much money to spend on a gift (because spending too much or too little can be embarrassing), parents may ask, "What's the going rate?" It is OK to ask other parents but if possible, try not to ask the parent of the child whose party it is. However, it is fine to ask if the child is particularly interested or "into" something, to give you an idea of what would be a welcome gift.

People may say, "We don't want anything", "No need for gifts" or "Don't bring anything, just yourselves". However, the guest who didn't actually take anything may be judged impolite. A small inexpensive gift is better than no gift.

A gift is traditionally wrapped in wrapping paper with a tag attached saying who it is for and from. Gifts are given on arrival to the person who is celebrating. A card may also be given. They are then put in one place and opened after the party. You can expect to receive a thank you note.

It is polite for parent and child to say, "Thank you" after a party, play date or a lift in a car. The child says, "Thank you for having me". A parent may also follow it up with a text saying how much the child enjoyed their time.

It's best to try to avoid anything other than positive comments about other people's children. Criticism of a child is only really allowed by their own parents. Dealing with "bad behaviour" can be a problem because different families have different beliefs about what is good or bad behaviour. English people are sometimes surprised by other English children's behaviour. It is also worth knowing that, if a child's parents are separated, each parent may have different beliefs about what is good or bad behaviour. Also, there is an increasing understanding of, and respect for, children with learning difficulties or disabilities and that these may perhaps affect behaviour. If there is clearly "bad behaviour" and a parent is not present, it's OK to correct the child but it is not usually OK to punish them. If the parent is present, it's probably better to tell the parent.

| Words and phrases | Meaning |
|---|---|
| Little one, kid, tot, youngster, nipper | Child |
| Monkey/Cheeky monkey | A child who behaves mischievously |
| Youth | Teenage or young person |
| Tearaway | Teenager or young person who does silly/illegal things |
| Child's play | Very easy |
| A piece of cake | Very easy |
| A walk in the park | Very easy |
| Mother hen | A mother who is extremely protective of her child |
| Were you born in a barn? | Close the door, please |

| Words and phrases used by teenagers and young people (These change quickly. The online www.urbandictionary.com is usually up to date) | Meaning |
|---|---|
| Sick | Very good |
| Buff | Well-groomed |

| Jarring | Annoying |
|---|---|
| A beast, a legend | A person who has done something that is funny or helpful |
| Peak | Unfair or bad |
| Hench | Muscular |
| Owned | Embarrassed or humiliated |
| Fam | Close friends (can be family members) |
| Lit | Good, fun |
| Bare | A lot of |

*"I'd never heard of a "lollipop lady". To me it's so funny, maybe it's the shape of the stick they hold. Everyone should know about lollipop ladies, they help you to cross the road." Anon.*

# 9. Festivals and Traditions

**Christmas** is celebrated on 25th December. This Christian festival to mark the birth of Jesus is also celebrated by some non-Christians by spending time with family, sharing gifts and going to parties in the weeks before and after 25th December.

The 6th January is known as the Epiphany and marks the presenting of gifts to Jesus. It is considered bad luck to celebrate Christmas beyond this date.

Greetings and goodbyes around this time include, "Merry Christmas" and "Happy Christmas".

Traditionally, infants and primary school children perform a re-enactment of the story of Jesus' birth. This is called a "nativity play" or "nativity". Christian Christmas songs are called "carols".

**Father Christmas** is a character (dressed in red) who enters every child's house after they go to sleep on 24th December. Also known as Santa or Santa Claus, he leaves gifts for them to open in the morning. Before Christmas, children are asked, "What do you want from Father Christmas?" and from 25th December onwards children are asked, "What did Father Christmas bring you?".

Gifts and cards are exchanged between people who want to offer their best wishes for the Christmas season. Family, friends and neighbours may be included. A gift for a colleague, a teacher or house staff (cleaner/dog walker/ nanny) is not expected, although some people do. It is considered polite to thank a person who has sent a card or a gift.

Christmas decorations are on display any time from the middle of November in homes, shops, schools and hospitals and some shopping streets. The appearance of Christmas gifts in the shops earlier and earlier each year is an English topic of conversation. Decorations usually include a Christmas tree adorned with seasonal decorations and fairy lights, colourful shiny items such as tinsel and sometimes a wreath on the exterior of the front door.

**A traditional Christmas** meal is shared with as many family members as possible.

A Christmas cracker is placed on each person's table-place. Two people pull the cracker ends until it splits into two parts (which creates a bang/snap noise). The person with the larger part of the cracker wins the contents: a paper hat to wear during the meal, a toy or gadget and a joke. It is traditional to read the jokes aloud at the table during the meal.

Before people start to eat, a senior person around the table may lead a tribute to absent family and friends. This is known as a "toast".

The actual meal is usually served in the afternoon of the 25th. It typically includes roast turkey with stuffing, roast potatoes and a variety of vegetables including sprouts. Also traditional are miniature sausages wrapped in bacon known as "pigs in blankets", gravy, bread sauce and cranberry sauce. Christmas pudding is served warm with brandy butter. A trifle and a yule log are also customary.

**Pantomimes** are family-friendly theatre productions during the Christmas season. They are based on a traditional fairy tale and with a lot of laughter at strange behaviour and jokes.

**Shrove Tuesday** is also known as "Pancake Day", with its roots in Christian preparations for Easter; this day is when pancakes are made, flipped and eaten.

**Easter** is a Christian festival which runs from Palm Sunday to Easter Sunday. It marks and celebrates the passion, crucifixion, and resurrection of Jesus. Some Christians and non-Christians celebrate Easter by exchanging chocolate eggs on Easter Sunday. This is particularly popular with children because an Easter Bunny leaves eggs for well-behaved children. Bunnies represent new life. A traditional Easter Egg Hunt usually takes place in a garden or park with children finding the hidden eggs. Easter dates vary.

**Bonfire Night** is celebrated annually on 5th November with fireworks, sparklers and sometimes a bonfire. It marks 'The Gunpowder Plot' of 1605 when Guy Fawkes and others tried to blow up the Houses of Parliament in London.

---

### A Traditional Bonfire Night Rhyme

*"Remember, remember, the fifth of November,*

*Gunpowder, treason and plot.*

*I see no reason why gunpowder treason,*

*Should ever be forgot."*

---

**St Patrick's Day** (people wear lots of green coloured clothing)**, St Andrew's Day, St David's Day, Eid, Chinese New Year, Diwali, Hanukkah, Purim, Vaisakhi, Holi, Norouz, Thanksgiving and Wesak, Gay Pride/ LGBT Pride and other national days of charity and awareness** are celebrated in England to varying degrees depending on people and place.

**Charity Days** for high-profile charities include, "Children in Need" and "Macmillan's Coffee Morning" and the biannual "Comic Relief'" and "Sport Relief". These feature on radio and TV and many schools, hospitals and businesses raise money for charities (known as, "good causes").

**Bank Holidays** are public holidays. There are eight a year. Public buildings and many businesses close. Public transport is usually affected.

**Good luck** symbols include a horseshoe, a black cat and four-leaf clover/shamrock. Some people believe that touching wood brings protection and say "touch wood". To wish someone good luck, the expression is "fingers crossed" and the gesture is of the first two fingers crossed. A bride wears, "Something old, something new, something borrowed, something blue" on her wedding day for good luck.

**Unlucky** symbols include seeing one magpie (bird). Some people believe that walking under a ladder, breaking a mirror or putting new shoes on a table brings bad luck. The number 13 is widely considered unlucky. Hotels do not have a 13th floor. Some hospitals do not have number 13 wards or beds and some streets do not have house number 13. Friday 13th of any month is considered the unluckiest date.

# 10. Shopping and Eating Out

*"There is so much butter in sandwiches here!" Marina*

**Queuing** is the classic English stereotype and it is often true to reality. Good manners and being fair mean that it is polite to join the back of the line. Queue-jumping is not acceptable. The principle of "first come, first served" is very important to most English people. Space between people should be at least ten inches, and more where possible. Older people and women tend to like more space. Conversation between strangers in a queue is not common. Occasionally, for example in a supermarket queue, a person in front with lots of shopping may invite a person behind to go in front. It's not respectful to accept the offer if there are other shoppers in the queue behind. However, if the invitation is accepted, to say "Thank you very much" a few times is polite. People will queue when waiting for most things. If it is not clear whether there is a queue or not, a polite question is, "Sorry, are you waiting?". There are also queues without lines, for example, in bars and pubs, at lifts and hotel front-desks.

Electronic queues with ticket machines identify positions

in a queue.

> *"You don't want to push in a line [a queue]. People do get angry and say, 'Get to the back of the queue.'"*
> *Ewan*

**Please and thank you** are essential when shopping or

eating out. It is polite to treat all workers with respect

regardless of their status.

**Shopping** for clothes, food and other personal items

is done at local shops, markets or big supermarkets.

Department stores have a wider range of products.

Charity shops (shops that sell products to raise money for

charities) accept donations of unwanted and second-hand

items and sell at reduced prices. There is an increasing

number of "out-of-town" shopping centres/retail parks.

On-line shopping is also increasing. Traditionally many

shops are closed on Sundays. Large shops are not

allowed to trade for more than six hours between 10:00

and 18:00 on Sunday and are not allowed to open on Easter Sunday or on Christmas Day.

**Car parking** rules depend on location. It's a good idea to have some coins ready. Some parking payment machines accept credit card payment through mobile phones. Symbols painted on the ground show premium parking spaces available for people with disabilities or with children.

**Bus routes** usually include shopping and eating areas. It is polite to thank the bus driver at the end of the journey. Adult and child fares are usually different. Most bus companies offer discounts for a weekly bus pass. The female state pension age is the age that male and female passengers can get free bus travel. A person's pension age depends on their date of birth and can be calculated on the government website.

**Touching** non-food items while choosing what to buy is allowed by adults. Children are not encouraged to touch anything in shops. Most clothes shops have male or female only changing-rooms to try on clothes. A ticket may be provided and it is polite to leave the changing-room tidy. Shoes and coats are tried on in the general shopping area. Items in packages should be taken to a shop assistant who can help to unwrap the item for inspection.

**Returning** unwanted items depends on each shop's policy. Broken/faulty items that were "not fit for purpose" will be refunded (it's the law). Returning items that don't fit is normal but a receipt is usually needed for a full refund.

**Eating out** can be in a café, takeaway or restaurant. Takeaways that also have dining areas are not usually called restaurants. Cafés are casual and sometimes people use laptops and other mobile devices in cafés. Restaurants range from casual to formal fine-dining.

The general rules of queuing and saying "Please" and "Thank you" when ordering and receiving are good manners.

**Table manners** start with not being too loud. It is impolite for a person to click their fingers to get a waiter's attention. Flirtatious or sexual advances towards staff are unacceptable. Place the closed menu on the table to signal "ready to order". The knife is held in the right hand, the fork in the left. Place both knife and fork in the middle of the plate to signal to the waiter, "Finished eating". Other impolite behaviour includes: eating with one's mouth open, blowing one's nose into napkins, licking knives and making a signing gesture to ask for the bill. Some restaurants allow e-cigarettes but other diners tend to dislike them being used. Using mobile phones is not really good manners but many people do.

*"The younger people are using their mobile phones at the table. You can see the parents getting upset. There are lots of different ways of child-rearing. There is diversity in the culture and you see it in the restaurant." Alexandhros*

**Tipping** 10% of the total bill in a restaurant is acceptable if the service is satisfactory. Sometimes the tip is included in the bill as "service charge". Café and takeaway staff do not expect tips.

*"Tips don't always get shared out. Sometimes only a small percentage goes to the waiter." Alexandhros*

**Hygiene and Food Safety** for most cafes, takeaways, restaurants and hotels are monitored and regulated by Local Authorities. Supermarkets and shops that sell food are also monitored and regulated.

**Tax/VAT** on shopping and services is usually 20% of the total price. It is normal to see VAT included in the price shown in shops. There is no VAT on children's clothes or on most food. Sometimes VAT is shown on a different line of a bill or receipt.

| Words and phrases | Meaning |
|---|---|
| Window-shopping | Looking without intending to buy |
| On the house | Paid for by the owner (usually of the bar or restaurant) |
| Tab | An amount of money that a named person owes in restaurant or bar and will pay later. "Put it on my tab" |
| Go Dutch | Two different meanings<br><br>1. To divide the cost of the bill between two people<br><br>2. To divide the cost of the bill equally between all of the people at the table |

# 11. Social Media

**Facebook, Twitter, Instagram, YouTube, Snapchat, WhatsApp and Pinterest** dominate social media. They are used to maintain communication with family, friends and communities. They are also used to share information and to establish communication with new friends and communities.

Information shared includes writing and photography (including photographs of people), art and science, opinion and discussion, music and video.

Most public libraries offer free internet access. A general search for network providers gives a list of services and prices to choose from.

Approaching a stranger to be a social media "friend" is not good manners. It is considered polite to acknowledge other people's contributions and to not claim false ownership.

It is common to "Google" (search for information about them online) someone before or after meeting them. People may have separate personal and professional accounts.

Many people add "xx" at the end of their message or post. These are symbols of kisses. Friends often share these. It is unprofessional to add kisses in work related messages.

*"You can use Facebook and that to learn English, learn new words and grammar. We looked for information in Facebook, even before we arrived here, like how to find new people and opportunities."*
*Marina*

**Age** of users, officially, is twelve years but under 12-year-olds sometimes have access. Schools incorporate online safety awareness into their teaching.

Official alerts and advice for people involved in (or close to) large-scale disasters such as flood, terrorism, fire or landslides are communicated through social media.

**Broken** computers, laptops, tablets and phones can be repaired at retailers or computer/phone repair shops. There are also online services that arrange to meet for repairs.

**Laws** are being developed. As a general rule, what is illegal in the physical environment is illegal in the virtual environment. This includes libel, harassment, incitement to violence, theft, abuse, indecency and breach of orders.

**Criminal** and very offensive posts can be reported to the social network website and to the police © 101. This includes hate crime. Some police areas have dedicated social media crime staff. People are generally encouraged to report crimes.

*"When we learn a new word, we use it in our posts."*
*Fatima*

| Words and phrases | Meaning |
| --- | --- |
| Swipe | Move fingertips across touch-screen |
| Profile | Personal data, image |
| Catfish | A false profile |
| Ping | To make contact by text message |
| Post | Something put online (image, writing) |
| Footprint | Identifiable set of unique actions |
| Like | To show interest in someone's content |
| Tag | To link to another person |
| Follow | To subscribe to updates |
| Unplug | To stop using social media for some time |
| Friend | To add a person to a list of contacts |
| Block | To prevent contact |
| Viral | Popularity gained by users sharing |
| Cloud | Storage and processing space |
| Troll | A person who starts arguments or posts insulting comments |

# 12. Sport

**Sports news** is usually towards the end of the national news on TV and radio and is found on the back pages of national and local newspapers. Information about local sports groups and clubs can be found on the internet and in local newspapers.

Joining a local club can help people to make friends and become accepted into the community.

*"I put my son into a local football team when he was in primary school. I coached and that way I made lots of friends; it helped me to feel safe, safe in the community. People knew me through the football and I became one of them. Football is big, football unites people."* Ali

**Participation** in sport or watching sport is enjoyed by more than half of the population. Women can participate freely. Cricket is officially the national sport. England's biggest rivals are Australia. However, football rather than cricket is the most popular sport. It is not called 'soccer'

in conversation. There are football clubs for children, men and women. Professional or amateur football is played in almost every community in the country. Support for a professional league team is usually a lifelong passion and feelings are usually very strong. A match/game between two neighbouring clubs is called a "derby". It is unacceptable for a foreigner to criticise the national team but English people can and often do. England's biggest rivals are Germany.

Some people believe that sport is about winning and others believe that sport is about being involved. Some perspectives value non-competitive participation and others play to win.

**"Sportsmanship"** is a principle that is traditionally important and for some people it still is. It means that when playing sport, there should be a desire to win and fairness towards opponents. Shaking hands is a symbol of good "sportsmanship". Another example is helping an opponent who has fallen. Children, men and women are expected to show "sportsmanship". Examples of bad sportsmanship are pretending to be injured or excessive celebrations when gaining points or scores.

An **"underdog"** is often favoured. This individual or team is least likely to win but supporters/fans from other clubs will support the "underdog". The sporting principle of fairness and "anyone can win" is why the "underdog" is so appealing. The "underdog" can also be supported in other environments such as places of work or education.

**Social patterns** exist in sport. For example, polo and rowing are more exclusive than basketball and darts. Tennis, golf and rugby, netball, horse-racing, fishing (angling), snooker, athletics, cycling, badminton, bowls, boxing, swimming, martial arts are also played throughout the country.

**Uniting people** through sport is the main reason why the London 2012 Olympics were regarded as successful. For 'Team GB', 24 of the 65 medals were won by people who themselves or their family came from another country.

When celebrating success for the UK or for Team GB all

of the four nations (England, Northern Ireland, Scotland

and Wales) are united in pride.

| Words and phrases | Meaning |
|---|---|
| A good sport | A person who is relaxed about doing something that may be embarrassing |
| To have the upper hand | In a position of advantage and likely to win |
| Neck and neck | To be exactly equal during a competition/ match |
| A tie | More than one winner at end of a competition/ match |
| A sitting duck | Easily attacked |

# Useful Websites and Telephone Numbers

Official UK Government website **www.gov.uk**

Emergency (police, ambulance or fire) 📞 999 or 📞 112

( 📞 112 will work on a locked mobile phone)

Non-emergency Police 📞 101

Non-emergency medical help 📞 111

National Health Service. NHS England.

**www.england.nhs.uk**

Free information 📞 0300 311 22 33

Find local services and Health & Lifestyle Advice

Symptom Checker at: **www.nhs.uk**

Healthwatch **www.healthwatch.co.uk**

Guidance for immigrants at: **www.gov.uk/guidance/nhs-entitlements-migrant-health-guide**

---

Citizens Advice **www.citizensadvice.org.uk**

Free advice on any matter

---

The Samaritans **www.samaritans.org**

Free 24 hour online or telephone help for anyone in emotional need ✆ 116 123

---

The Silver Line **www.thesilverline.org.uk**

Free 24-hour telephone help for older people

📞 0800 4 70 80 90

---

Childline **www.childline.org.uk**

Free online or 24-hour telephone help for
children 0-19 years 📞 0800 1111

---

Migrant Help UK **www.migranthelpuk.org**

Free advice for vulnerable migrants 📞 01304 203977

---

Shelter **www.england.shelter.org.uk**

Free online or telephone advice for anyone about housing

ACAS **www.acas.org.uk**

Free online or telephone advice for anyone about work
(includes a translation service) 🕿 0300 123 1100

---

Driver and Vehicle Licensing Agency **www.gov.uk/
government/organisations/driver-and-vehicle-
licensing-agency**

The Highway Code **www.gov.uk/guidance/the-highway-
code**

Driving Licence **www.gov.uk/driving-nongb-licence**

---

Online discussion forum for parents **www.mumsnet.com**

---

Online dictionary of new words
**www.urbandictionary.com**

# Quiz

Do you think these statements are true or false?

Check online at **www.englishunwrapped.com**

---

1. It is polite to say "please" when asking for anything.
   **True or False**

---

2. English humour can include laughing at oneself.
   **True or False**

---

3. Everyone in England lives in a big beautiful clean house with a garden.
   **True or False**

---

4. "Snowed under" means to be under a pile of snow.
   **True or False**

---

5. Most children in England have a hot meal in the middle of the school day.
   **True or False**

---

6. All healthcare is free for everyone in England.

   **True or False**

---

7. "Bobby" is a slang word for "a policeman."

   **True or False**

---

8. "Were you born in a barn?" means "Close the door, please."

   **True or False**

---

9. The number thirteen is considered unlucky.

   **True or False**

---

10. Café and takeaway staff expect a 10% tip.

    **True or False**

---

11. All public libraries offer free internet access.

    **True or False**

---

12. Football is the most popular sport.

    **True or False**

---

13. The laws are the same in England, Wales, Scotland and Northern Ireland

    **True or False**

---

Check your answers online at
**www.englishunwrapped.com**

www.englishunwrapped.com